Best Cookies

SAVEUR

Swiss raspberry sandwich cookies.

Best Cookies

50 Classic Recipes

SAVEUR

BY THE EDITORS OF SAVEUR MAGAZINE

weldon**owen**

An assortment of antique Swedish cookie cutters.

TABLE OF CONTENTS

INTRODUCTION

Cookies are what childhood memories are made of. In fact, helping bake them and decorate them is the very first thing many of us learned to do in the kitchen. Cookies are simply the ultimate homemade treat, no matter where you live. The quick, easy recipes in this book come from all over the world: cream-filled wafer cookies from Norway, pecan shortbreads from Mexico, butter cookies from France, maple-walnut squares from Quebec, snickerdoodles from the American heartland, and so many more. They range from the simple and homey to the ethereal and elegant, from classic peanut butter cookies and brownies to orange-scented meringue kisses and anise-infused biscotti. None of these recipes requires fancy ingredients, expensive equipment, or complicated techniques. After all, cookies are supposed to be as fun to make as they are to eat, and we want you to use these recipes again and again, to hang on to them and pass them on to your friends, your kids, and your grandkids. Because everybody knows that there's no better way to say "I love you" than with a batch of freshly baked cookies. —*THE EDITORS*

Becky Ferris, a home cook in Remsen, New York, sifts ingredients for holiday baking.

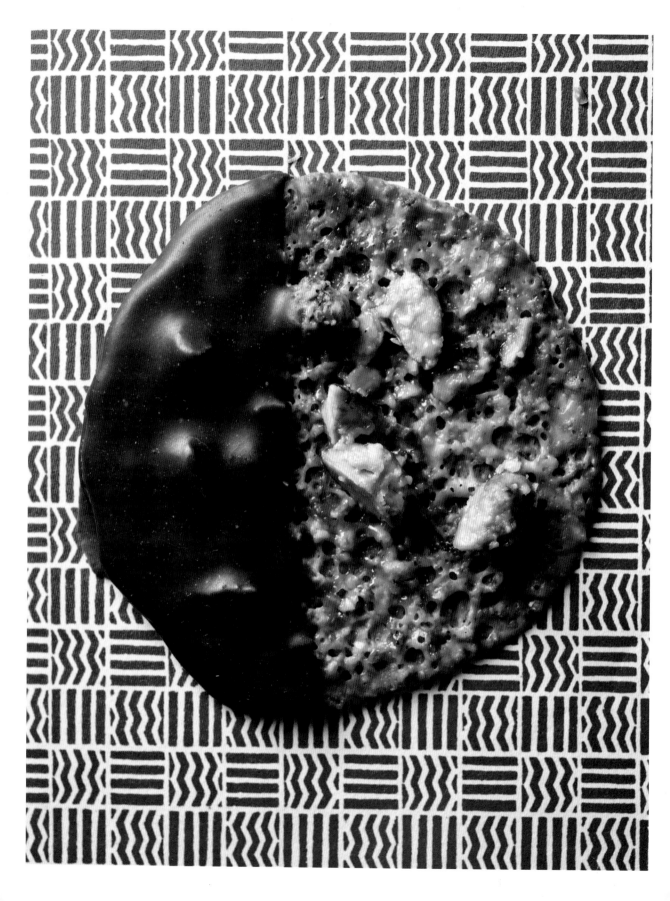

CHOCOLATE-DIPPED PISTACHIO FLORENTINES

MAKES ABOUT 8 DOZEN

A glossy coating of chocolate makes these famously buttery,
crunchy wafer cookies even more sumptuous.

FOR THE COOKIES:

- ¾ cup heavy cream
- 1 cup sugar
- 4 tbsp. unsalted butter
- 3 tbsp. flour
- 2 cups sliced pistachios
- 1½ cups finely ground pistachios
- 2 tsp. vanilla extract

FOR THE GLAZE:

- ½ cup sugar
- 3 tbsp. light corn syrup
- 4 oz. semisweet chocolate, preferably 54%, roughly chopped

1 Make the cookies: Bring cream, sugar, and butter to a boil in a 2-qt. saucepan over medium-high heat, stirring to dissolve sugar. Remove from heat, and stir in flour; add sliced and ground pistachios and vanilla and stir until evenly combined.

2 Heat oven to 350°. Spoon teaspoon-size portions of the batter onto parchment paper–lined baking sheets, spacing the portions 3" apart. Bake until cookies are golden brown and set, about 10 minutes. Let cool completely.

3 Meanwhile, make the glaze: Bring sugar, corn syrup, and 3 tbsp. water to a boil in a 1-qt. saucepan over high heat. Remove from heat, add chocolate, and swirl pan to coat the chocolate with the sugar mixture. Let sit without stirring to allow the chocolate to melt, about 5 minutes. Stir chocolate with a rubber spatula until smooth; let cool slightly.

4 Dip half of each cookie into the chocolate glaze. Transfer to a sheet of parchment paper and let the glaze solidify.

ANISE, ALMOND, AND HAZELNUT BISCOTTI

(Tozzetti)

MAKES 40

These nutty, anise-flavored biscotti, a Roman specialty, are made from a batter that is poured onto a baking sheet and baked like a cake.

	Butter, for greasing pan
3½	cups flour, plus more for pan
1	tbsp. baking powder
2	cups whole blanched almonds, toasted
1½	cups whole blanched hazelnuts, toasted
2¼	cups sugar
5	eggs
¼	cup anise-flavored liqueur, like sambuca
1	tbsp. crushed anise seeds
1	tbsp. vanilla extract

1 Heat oven to 375°. Grease a 10" x 15" jelly roll pan and dust with flour; set aside. In a bowl, whisk together the flour and baking powder; add nuts and toss to combine. In a separate bowl, whisk together sugar and eggs until smooth; whisk in sambuca, anise seeds, and vanilla. Add flour mixture, and fold until smooth. Pour into pan, and bake until golden, 20 minutes; let cool.

2 Reduce oven temperature to 325°. Invert pan to remove biscotti slab, and cut crosswise into about twenty 10"-long strips; cut each strip in half to form forty 5"-long strips. Transfer strips to parchment paper–lined baking sheets, spacing strips 2" apart. Bake until golden brown, about 20–25 minutes. Let cool.

Baking Tip *Don't crowd the biscotti on the baking sheet when baking for the second time. If you do, they will steam rather than toast.*

CLASSIC SUGAR COOKIES

MAKES ABOUT 2 DOZEN LARGE COOKIES

These are the cookies Christmas memories are made of. Cut them into any
festive shapes you like and decorate them with icing, sprinkles, or sugar
or all of the above. Or just eat them right out of the oven.

6 cups flour

1½ tsp. baking powder

1 tsp. kosher salt

3 cups sugar

1½ cups (3 sticks) unsalted butter, softened

1 tbsp. vanilla extract

3 eggs

Royal icing, sprinkles, and sanding sugars, for decorating

1 Whisk together flour, baking powder, and salt in a bowl; set aside. In an electric mixer fitted with a paddle, beat together sugar, butter, and vanilla until fluffy. Add eggs one at a time, beating after each addition. Add the reserved flour mixture; beat to combine. Transfer dough to a floured surface; divide into 4 pieces. Shape each piece into a flat disk. Wrap each disk in plastic, and refrigerate for 1 hour.

2 Heat oven to 325°. Working with 1 disk at a time, roll to a ⅛" thickness on a floured surface. Using cookie cutters of your choice, cut out shapes and place cookies on parchment paper–lined baking sheets, spacing cookies 2" apart. Reroll dough scraps and repeat. Bake until lightly browned, 12–15 minutes. Let cool. Decorate with royal icing, sprinkles, and sugars.

Baking Tip *When making large, fragile shapes such as snowflakes or candy canes, use a wide metal offset spatula to transfer the cut dough pieces to the baking sheets.*

BACI DI DAMA

MAKES ABOUT 3 DOZEN

These hazelnut-meringue sandwich cookies, filled with milk chocolate, are known as "lady's kisses" in Italy.

6   oz. blanched whole hazelnuts

1   cup sugar

½   tsp. kosher salt

⅓   cup cornstarch

2   egg whites

4   oz. milk chocolate, melted

1 Heat oven to 325°. Place hazelnuts, ½ cup of the sugar, and the salt in a food processor, and process until nuts are finely ground. Transfer to a bowl, and stir in cornstarch; set aside. Beat egg whites in a large bowl with an electric mixer on high speed until soft peaks form; slowly add remaining sugar, and beat until stiff peaks form. Add hazelnut mixture, and gently fold with a rubber spatula until evenly combined.

2 Transfer batter to a piping bag fitted with a ⅜" plain tip, and pipe about 3 dozen ½"-wide mounds of batter onto parchment paper–lined baking sheets. Bake until lightly browned, about 16 minutes.

3 Place about ¼ tsp. melted chocolate on the flat side of 1 cookie, and top with another cookie; repeat with remaining cookies and chocolate. Let chocolate set before serving, about 5 minutes.

Baking Tip *Resist the urge to overfill these cookie sandwiches. If you do, they won't set properly and the chocolate will overflow at the edges.*

BLUEBERRY POPPY SEED SQUARES

(Borůvkový Koláč)

MAKES 1 DOZEN

Poppy seeds, with their earthy and floral flavors, are a key ingredient in many Central and Eastern European sweets, including these Czech dessert bars.

20	tbsp. unsalted butter, softened, plus more for pan
3	cups flour, plus more for pan
1½	cups sugar
¾	tsp. kosher salt
¼	tsp. vanilla extract
4	cups blueberries
2	tbsp. fresh lemon juice
½	tsp. ground cinnamon
1½	cups ground poppy seeds
½	cup heavy cream

1 Heat oven to 350°. Grease a 9" x 13" metal baking pan and dust with flour; set aside. Beat 16 tbsp. of the butter and ½ cup of the sugar with an electric mixer on medium-high speed until pale and fluffy, about 2 minutes. Add 2½ cups of the flour and ½ tsp. of the salt; beat until just combined and a dough forms. Transfer the dough to the prepared pan and press it into the bottom and halfway up the sides of the pan; refrigerate for 20 minutes. Bake the crust until lightly browned, about 12 minutes; let cool.

2 Meanwhile, add the remaining butter, flour, and salt, plus ¼ cup of the sugar and the vanilla, in a bowl and stir until coarse crumbs form; set streusel topping aside.

3 Heat remaining sugar, 3 cups of the blueberries, the lemon juice, and the cinnamon in a 2-qt. saucepan over medium-high heat; cook until berries burst, about 20 minutes. Remove from heat, and stir in remaining berries; let cool. Stir together poppy seeds and cream in a bowl; spread poppy seed mixture evenly over cooled crust. Pour blueberry mixture over poppy seed mixture; sprinkle with streusel topping.

4 Bake until filling is bubbly and streusel is lightly browned, about 40 minutes. Let cool, and cut into squares.

Baking Tip *Purchase ground poppy seeds or grind your own with a poppy seed grinder, both available at Amazon.com.*

BROWNED-BUTTER THUMBPRINTS

MAKES ABOUT 4 DOZEN

These dainty cookies are baked with browned butter, which gives
them a warm, nutty flavor that contrasts beautifully
with the tangy lime curd in the cookie's center.

FOR THE COOKIES:

16 tbsp. unsalted butter

1 cup sugar

2 cups flour

½ tsp. kosher salt

FOR THE LIME CURD:

⅓ cup sugar

1 tbsp. lime zest

3 egg yolks

1 egg

½ cup fresh lime juice

1 tbsp. unsalted butter,
   cubed and chilled

1 Make the cookies: Heat butter in a small saucepan over medium heat until its solids begin to brown and smell nutty; pour into a small bowl, scraping bottom of pan to release any browned bits, and refrigerate until solid. Place solidified brown butter in a bowl along with the sugar, and beat with a hand mixer on high speed until fluffy, about 3 minutes. Add flour and salt and beat on low speed until just combined. Using a 1-oz. ice cream scoop or 2 tablespoons, portion and shape dough into 1" balls and place on parchment paper–lined baking sheets, spacing balls 2" apart. Using your index finger or the end of a wooden spoon, press down on the dough balls to flatten them slightly and create a deep well; refrigerate cookies until well-chilled, at least 1 hour.

2 Meanwhile, make the lime curd: Whisk together sugar, lime zest, egg yolks, and egg in a 2-qt. saucepan until smooth; whisk in lime juice, and heat over medium heat. Cook, stirring constantly, until mixture thickens to the consistency of loose pudding; remove from heat, add butter, and whisk until smooth. Transfer to a small bowl and press a piece of plastic wrap directly on the surface of the curd; refrigerate until well-chilled, at least 2 hours.

3 Heat oven to 375°. Bake cookies, rotating baking sheets top to bottom and front to back halfway through cooking, until dry to the touch and golden brown on the bottom, about 16 minutes; let cool completely. When ready to serve, use a spoon to fill cavities of each cookie with some of the lime curd and serve immediately.

Baking Tip *When pressing the holes in the cookies, dip your finger or the end of a wooden spoon in flour after each use to keep it from sticking to the dough.*

BLONDIES

MAKES 1 DOZEN

This all-American dessert, a cousin of the brownie, has a rich flavor that's closer to caramel than to chocolate. Substitute butterscotch for the white chocolate, if you like.

12	tbsp. unsalted butter, melted, plus more for pan
2	cups flour, plus more for pan
1½	tsp. baking powder
¼	tsp. kosher salt
1¼	cups packed light brown sugar
½	cup sugar
1	tsp. vanilla extract
2	eggs
2	cups roughly chopped white chocolate

1 Heat oven to 350°. Grease a 9" x 13" baking pan and dust with flour; set aside. Whisk together flour, baking powder, and salt; set aside. Whisk together sugars, vanilla, and eggs in a bowl until smooth. Add the butter, and stir until smooth. Add the flour mixture, and stir until just combined.

2 Stir in white chocolate, and spread batter in the prepared pan. Bake until a toothpick inserted in the middle comes out with a few crumbs attached, about 20 minutes. Let cool, and cut into squares.

CHOCOLATE CHOCOLATE-CHIP COOKIES

MAKES ABOUT 5 DOZEN

These dense, chewy cookies, enriched with cocoa powder and
two kinds of chocolate, are a chocolate-lover's dream.

2	cups flour
1	cup natural cocoa powder
1	tsp. kosher salt
1	tsp. baking powder
½	tsp. baking soda
1	cup sugar
¾	cup light brown sugar
8	tbsp. unsalted butter, softened
4	eggs
2	tsp. vanilla extract
2	cups roughly chopped bittersweet chocolate
2	cups roughly chopped milk chocolate

1 Heat oven to 350°. Whisk together flour, cocoa powder, salt, baking powder, and baking soda in a medium bowl; set aside. Combine both sugars and the butter in a large bowl and beat with an electric mixer on medium-high speed until pale and fluffy, about 3 minutes. Add eggs, one at a time, beating after each addition, until mixture is smooth. Beat in vanilla, and then add the reserved flour mixture; beat until just combined. Add both chocolates, and stir until evenly combined.

2 Divide the dough into 1-oz. portions and roll them into balls. Place balls 2" apart on parchment paper–lined baking sheets, and bake until just set but still slightly underdone in the middle, about 10 minutes. Let cool completely before serving.

CARAMEL CRUMB BARS

MAKES ABOUT 3 DOZEN

These caramel-and-streusel-topped shortbread cookies
are a year-round favorite in New Zealand.

20	tbsp. unsalted butter, softened, plus more for pan
2½	cups flour, plus more for pan
½	cup sugar
1	tsp. vanilla extract
¼	tsp. kosher salt
¼	cup packed dark brown sugar
1	tbsp. light corn syrup
1	14-oz. can sweetened condensed milk

1 Heat oven to 350°. Line a 9" x 13" baking pan with parchment paper; grease baking sheet and dust with flour. In an electric mixer fitted with a paddle, beat together 16 tbsp. butter, sugar, vanilla, and salt until fluffy. Add 2¼ cups of flour, and beat until smooth. Transfer ¾ of the dough to the prepared baking pan; press dough into bottom of the pan and refrigerate. Rub remaining dough and flour together in your hands to create large crumbs for the streusel topping; set aside.

2 Combine remaining butter, brown sugar, corn syrup, and condensed milk in a 2-qt. saucepan. Cook, stirring, over medium-high heat until caramel forms, 8–10 minutes. Pour caramel over the dough on the baking pan; scatter the streusel crumbs over top.

3 Bake until golden, 25–30 minutes. Let cool, and cut into bars.

CHERRY-ALMOND
STAR COOKIES
MAKES ABOUT 4 DOZEN

Infused with cherry brandy and enriched with cream,
these cherry-topped Italian-style cookies are a festive treat.

3	cups flour
2	tsp. baking powder
½	tsp. kosher salt
12	tbsp. unsalted butter, softened
1	cup sugar
¾	cup (7 oz.) almond paste
2	eggs
¼	cup heavy cream
1	tbsp. kirsch (cherry brandy)
1	tsp. vanilla extract
	Maraschino cherries, to garnish

1 Whisk together flour, baking powder, and salt in a bowl; set aside. In a medium bowl, beat butter and sugar with an electric mixer on medium speed until pale and fluffy, about 2 minutes; set aside. In a large bowl, beat almond paste at medium speed until smooth; add ¼ of the butter-sugar mixture, and beat until smooth. Add remaining butter-sugar mixture, and beat until smooth. Add eggs one at a time, beating well after each addition, until evenly combined. Add cream, kirsch, and vanilla, and beat until smooth. Add reserved flour mixture, and beat until just combined.

2 Transfer dough to a piping bag fitted with a ½" star tip, and pipe 2" mounds of dough onto parchment paper–lined baking sheets, spacing the cookies 2" apart. Halve the maraschino cherries, and place a cherry half atop each cookie; refrigerate cookies for 30 minutes.

3 Heat oven to 375°. Bake cookies, rotating baking sheets top to bottom and front to back halfway through cooking, until lightly browned, about 14 minutes.

Baking Tip *Piping the dough for these cookies will be easier if the dough is at room temperature.*

RUGELACH

MAKES ABOUT 3 DOZEN

In this version of the beloved Jewish pastry, cream cheese and sour cream
add richness to the dough. Use raspberry jam or melted chocolate
instead of apricot jam for two other classic variations.

4	tbsp. unsalted butter, softened
4	oz. cream cheese, softened
½	cup sour cream
1	egg
2¾	cups flour
¼	cup confectioners' sugar
¼	tsp. kosher salt
5	tbsp. sugar
1	tbsp. ground cinnamon
½	cup apricot jam
½	cup chopped walnuts
½	cup currants
1	egg, lightly beaten

1 Make the dough: In an electric mixer fitted with a
paddle, beat butter and cream cheese on medium speed.
Add sour cream and egg and continue beating until smooth.
Add flour, confectioners' sugar, and salt, and continue
beating mixture on low speed until a dough forms around
paddle. Divide dough into 4 balls and wrap each in plastic;
refrigerate for 1 hour.

2 Make the filling: Heat oven to 350°. Combine sugar and
cinnamon in a small bowl; set aside. Working with 1 dough
ball at a time, use a rolling pin to roll out a 10" circle. Spread
2 tbsp. of the apricot jam over the surface of the dough circle,
leaving a ¼" border around edges, and sprinkle the top with
1 tbsp. of the cinnamon-sugar mixture, 2 tbsp. of the walnuts,
and 2 tbsp. of the currants; press down on the filling lightly
with your hands.

3 Using a knife, cut dough circle into 10 wedges, as you
would a pizza. Working with 1 wedge at a time, roll up
the dough from wide end to narrow end. Transfer rolled
crescent to a parchment paper–lined baking sheet; repeat
with remaining dough balls, jam, cinnamon-sugar, mixture
walnuts, and currants.

4 Brush crescents with beaten egg and sprinkle with
remaining cinnamon-sugar. Bake, rotating baking sheets
halfway through cooking, until well browned, 20–25 minutes.
Transfer to a rack and let cool before serving.

Baking Tip *A pizza-cutting wheel works nicely for cutting
the dough circles into wedges.*

CHOCOLATE-ALMOND SPICE COOKIES

(Basler Brunsli)

MAKES ABOUT 4 DOZEN

Specialties of Basel, Switzerland, these chewy, flourless confections
unite chocolate and spice for a warm wintertime treat.

8	oz. whole blanched almonds
1½	cups sugar, plus more for rolling
6	oz. semisweet chocolate, finely chopped
1½	tsp. ground cinnamon
½	tsp. ground cloves
2	egg whites, lightly beaten

1 Add almonds and sugar to a food processor and process until nuts are finely ground. Add chocolate; pulse until finely ground. Add cinnamon, cloves, and egg whites; pulse to make a dough.

2 Sprinkle a large piece of parchment paper with sugar; transfer dough to the paper. Lay another piece of parchment paper over the dough; roll dough to a ⅛" thickness. Cut out cookies with a star-shaped cutter (or another shape of your choice); transfer to parchment paper–lined baking sheets, spacing cookies 1" apart. Reroll scraps and repeat. Let dough rest at room temperature for 3 hours.

3 Heat oven to 300°. Bake until cookies are slightly puffed, 12–15 minutes. Let cool completely before serving.

ITALIAN CHOCOLATE-ALMOND COOKIES

(Strazzate)

MAKES ABOUT 3 DOZEN

Popular in the Basilicata region of Italy, these crumbly cookies are flavored with herbal liqueur and are more nutty than sweet.

2	tbsp. unsalted butter, for greasing
½	tsp. baking powder
1¾	cups finely ground almonds, plus 2 tbsp. roughly chopped
1½	cups plus 2 tbsp. flour
1	cup sugar
2	tbsp. semisweet chocolate chips
1	tbsp. cocoa powder
1	tbsp. extra-virgin olive oil
½	tsp. kosher salt
½	cup Strega or Galliano liqueur
⅓	cup coffee, at room temperature

1 Heat oven to 325°. Grease 2 parchment paper–lined baking sheets and set aside. In a small bowl, whisk together baking powder and 1 tbsp. lukewarm water until dissolved, 20 seconds.

2 Combine ground and chopped almonds, flour, sugar, chocolate chips, cocoa powder, oil, and salt in a large bowl. With a wooden spoon, vigorously stir in the reserved baking powder mixture, the liqueur, and the coffee to form a wet dough.

3 Divide the dough into 1-oz. portions. Using your hands, roll dough portions into balls and transfer to prepared baking sheets, spacing the cookies about 1" apart. Bake until set, about 30 minutes. Transfer cookies to racks and let cool before serving.

COCONUT CANDY SQUARES

MAKES 2 DOZEN

The buttery graham cracker crust, the sweet coconut filling,
the chocolate–peanut butter glaze: This dessert is pure joy.

2   cups graham cracker crumbs

8   tbsp. unsalted butter, melted

½   cup sugar

2   cups sweetened shredded coconut

1   14-oz. can sweetened condensed milk

1   cup semisweet chocolate chips

2   tbsp. vegetable shortening

1   tbsp. creamy peanut butter

1 Heat oven to 350°. Stir together graham cracker crumbs, butter, and sugar in a medium bowl. Spread crumb mixture on the bottom of a 9" x 13" baking pan and press down with your fingers to form an even layer. Bake until just golden around the edges, 10–12 minutes. Set aside.

2 Put coconut and condensed milk into a bowl and stir well. Transfer the coconut mixture to the baking pan and spread it out evenly over the warm crust. Return pan to oven and bake until golden brown around the edges, 15–17 minutes. Let cool completely.

3 Put chocolate chips, vegetable shortening, and peanut butter into a medium pot and cook over medium-low heat, stirring constantly, until completely smooth, 3–4 minutes. Pour chocolate mixture over coconut layer in the baking pan and use a rubber spatula to spread it out in a thin, even layer. Let cool completely.

4 Cut into 24 squares. Serve, or layer between sheets of wax paper in an airtight container and refrigerate for up to 2 weeks.

COCONUT COOKIES
MAKES ABOUT 2 DOZEN

A cross between coconut macaroons and butter cookies, these moist, chewy treats make an excellent afternoon snack with tea or coffee.

2   cups unsweetened shredded coconut

½   cup sugar

1   tbsp. flour

4   tbsp. melted butter

2   egg yolks

1   whole egg

1 Heat oven to 350°. Mix coconut, sugar, flour, butter, egg yolks, and egg in a medium bowl until ingredients hold together.

2 Moisten your hands with water, and roll dough into walnut-size balls. Transfer dough balls to parchment paper–lined baking sheets, and bake until golden on top, about 15 minutes.

CORNMEAL COOKIES

(Paste di Meliga)

MAKES ABOUT 3 DOZEN

Cornmeal is widely eaten in northern Italy in the form of polenta,
but the ingredient also shows up in these lemon-kissed cookies,
sold in pastry shops all over the region.

2¼ cups flour

¾ cup yellow cornmeal

1 cup sugar

1 tsp. finely grated
lemon zest

1 cup, plus 5 tbsp. unsalted
butter, softened

2 egg yolks

1 Add flour, cornmeal, sugar, and lemon zest to a large bowl; stir to combine. Add butter and egg yolks. Using your fingers, work butter and egg yolks into the flour-cornmeal mixture until a soft dough forms. Turn dough out onto a clean surface and knead 4 or 5 times until smooth (dough will be soft and tacky). Cover dough with a clean, damp kitchen towel and let rest for 1 hour.

2 Heat oven to 300°. Transfer dough to a pastry bag fitted with a ⅜" star-shaped pastry tip. Pipe 2"-diameter spirals of dough out onto parchment paper–lined baking sheets, spacing the portions about 2" apart. Bake until edges turn pale golden brown, 20–25 minutes.

COWBOY COOKIES

MAKES ABOUT 2 DOZEN

True to its name, the cowboy cookie is rustic and adaptable—swap in almost any nutty or chocolaty ingredient you like—and incredibly satisfying. This recipe comes from former first lady Laura Bush.

¾ cup flour

¾ tsp. baking powder

¾ tsp. baking soda

¾ tsp. ground cinnamon

¼ tsp. kosher salt

6 tbsp. unsalted butter, softened

6 tbsp. sugar

6 tbsp. packed light brown sugar

1 egg

¾ tsp. vanilla extract

¾ cup rolled oats

¾ cup semisweet chocolate chips

½ cup chopped pecans

½ cup sweetened flaked coconut

1 Heat oven to 350°. In a bowl, whisk together flour, baking powder, baking soda, cinnamon, and salt; set aside. In a large bowl, beat butter with a handheld mixer until smooth. Add both sugars, and beat until fluffy. Add egg and vanilla; beat until smooth. Add the reserved flour mixture; beat until a dough forms. Stir in oats, chocolate, pecans, and coconut.

2 Form dough into walnut-sized balls, and transfer dough balls to 2 parchment paper–lined baking sheets, spacing dough balls 2" apart. Bake until cooked through, 16–18 minutes.

DULCE DE LECHE
SANDWICH COOKIES
(Alfajores)
MAKES 20 COOKIE SANDWICHES

Variations on this elegant cookie can be found throughout Latin America, but *alfajores* are associated above all with the cafés of Buenos Aires, Argentina.

1²⁄₃	cups cornstarch
1¼	cups flour
1	tsp. baking powder
²⁄₃	cup sugar
10	tbsp. unsalted butter, softened
1	tbsp. cognac or brandy
½	tsp. lemon zest
4	egg yolks
	Canned dulce de leche, for filling cookies

1 Heat oven to 350°. In a bowl, sift together cornstarch, flour, and baking powder; set aside. In an electric mixer fitted with a paddle, beat together sugar and butter until fluffy. Add cognac and lemon zest; beat until smooth. Add egg yolks one at a time, beating after each addition. Add reserved cornstarch mixture, and beat until smooth.

2 Transfer dough to a floured surface, and knead briefly; divide dough into 3 equal-size portions. Working with 1 dough portion at a time, roll dough to a ¼" thickness. Using a 2½" round cookie cutter, cut out cookies; transfer the cookies to parchment paper–lined baking sheets, spacing them 1" apart. Reroll scraps and repeat.

3 Bake until golden brown, 12–15 minutes. Let cool. Flip half the cookies over; top each inverted cookie with 1 heaping teaspoon of the dulce de leche. Top with the remaining cookies.

CREAM CHEESE–HAZELNUT BROWNIES

MAKES 16 BROWNIES

Toasted hazelnuts and cream cheese pair beautifully in the filling
for these dense, fudgy, and utterly fabulous brownies.

FOR THE FILLING:

- 4 oz. cream cheese, softened
- ¼ cup sugar
- 1 egg
- 2 tsp. fresh lemon juice
- ½ tsp. vanilla extract
- ¼ cup finely ground roasted hazelnuts

FOR THE BATTER:

- 1 cup semisweet chocolate chips
- 4 tbsp. butter, plus more for greasing
- ¾ cup flour, plus more for greasing
- 2 tbsp. Dutch-process cocoa powder
- ½ tsp. baking powder
- ¼ tsp. kosher salt
- ¾ cup sugar
- 2 eggs
- 1 tsp. vanilla extract
- ½ cup coarsely chopped roasted hazelnuts

1 Make the filling: Put cream cheese and sugar into a large mixing bowl and beat with an electric mixer on medium speed until smooth. Add egg, lemon juice, and vanilla, and continue beating until well mixed. Fold in hazelnuts with a rubber spatula. Cover with plastic wrap and refrigerate.

2 Make the batter: Heat oven to 350°. Melt chocolate and butter together in a metal bowl set over a pan of simmering water over medium heat. Remove pan and bowl from heat and set aside. Sift flour, cocoa, baking powder, and salt together into a medium bowl and set aside. Put sugar, eggs, and vanilla into a large mixing bowl, and beat with an electric mixer on medium speed until smooth and pale yellow, about 2 minutes. Beat in melted-chocolate mixture, then add flour mixture and continue beating until batter is smooth. Fold in hazelnuts with a rubber spatula.

3 Grease an 8" square cake pan and dust with flour. Spread half the batter into pan. Spread filling over the batter. Gently spread remaining batter over the filling. Run the tip of a rubber spatula through the layers in swirling patterns to create a marbled effect. Bake until a toothpick inserted in the center comes out nearly clean, about 40 minutes. Allow to cool before cutting into 2" squares.

CRISPY OATMEAL-RAISIN COOKIES

MAKES ABOUT 4 DOZEN

These cookies spread out thin and bake up crisp around the edges,
creating a pleasing contrast with the chewy raisins inside.

2	cups flour
2	tsp. ground cinnamon
1	tsp. baking soda
16	tbsp. unsalted butter, softened
1	cup packed light brown sugar
1	cup sugar
2	eggs
1½	cups rolled oats
1	cup raisins
1	tsp. vanilla extract

1 Heat oven to 350°. Whisk together flour, cinnamon, and baking soda in a bowl; set aside. Place butter and both sugars in the bowl of an electric mixer fitted with a paddle. Beat on medium-high speed until fluffy and smooth, about 5 minutes. Add eggs, one at a time, beating after each addition, and beat until mixture is completely smooth. Add the reserved flour mixture, and beat on low speed until the flour is just incorporated and batter is smooth. Add oats, raisins, and vanilla, and beat on low speed until just combined. Refrigerate dough for 30 minutes.

2 Shape dough into 1" balls. Place balls at least 2" apart on parchment paper–lined baking sheets. Working with one baking sheet at a time, bake cookies, rotating the sheet halfway through cooking, until they're golden brown and just set, 10–15 minutes. The outside edge should be just slightly darker than the middle of the cookies. Transfer the baking sheet to a wire rack and let cookies rest until they're cool enough to handle, about 10 minutes. Using a metal spatula, transfer cookies to wire rack to let cool completely before serving.

FRENCH BUTTER COOKIES

(Punitions)

MAKES ABOUT 5 DOZEN

These incomparably rich little cookies were popularized by the Parisian baker Lionel Poilâne, who said that grandmothers in his native Normandy used to put them in kids' lunches and call them "little punishments," hence their French name.

10	tbsp. salted butter, softened
½	cup sugar
1	egg
2	cups flour

1 Use a hand mixer on medium speed to beat together butter and sugar until pale and fluffy, 2–3 minutes. Add egg and beat until smooth. Add flour and mix on low speed until just combined. Transfer dough to a work surface and form into a ball; halve ball and form each half into a flat disk. Wrap disks separately in plastic wrap and refrigerate until chilled, 1 hour.

2 Heat oven to 350°. Transfer one disk to a lightly floured work surface; using a rolling pin, roll out to ¼" thickness. Using a 1½" round or fluted cookie cutter, cut out rounds and transfer them to parchment paper–lined baking sheets, spacing the rounds 1" apart. Repeat with remaining dough disk. Bake, rotating baking sheets top to bottom and front to back halfway through cooking, until cookies are set but not browned, 8–10 minutes. Let cool before serving.

Baking Tip *Use the best-quality salted butter you can find; in the States, Kerrygold is a good choice.*

HAMANTASCHEN
MAKES ABOUT 2 DOZEN

These delicious jam-filled pastries are traditionally served on the Jewish holiday of Purim, though they make a wonderful teatime snack year-round.

4	oz. cream cheese, softened
8	tbsp. unsalted butter, softened
¼	cup sugar
1	tsp. vanilla extract
¼	tsp. kosher salt
1	cup flour
2	tbsp. apricot preserves
2	tbsp. raspberry preserves
1	egg white, beaten

1 In a medium bowl, combine cream cheese, butter, sugar, vanilla, and salt, and beat with a hand mixer on medium speed until smooth and fluffy, about 2 minutes. Add flour, and beat until just combined. Transfer dough to a clean surface, and form into a thin disk. Wrap disk in plastic wrap, and refrigerate for 30 minutes.

2 Transfer dough disk to a floured work surface and roll to a ³⁄₁₆" thickness. Using a 2½" round cookie cutter, cut dough into rounds. Reroll scraps and repeat. Transfer the rounds to 2 parchment paper–lined baking sheets. Place about ½ tsp. of apricot preserves in the center of half the rounds; place about ½ tsp. of raspberry preserves in the center of the remaining rounds. Brush some egg white around the edges of each round. Fold in the edges of each round to form a triangular package, leaving a small opening at the top. Refrigerate the filled cookies for 30 minutes.

3 Heat oven to 350°. Bake cookies, one sheet at a time, until lightly browned, about 15 minutes. Let cool before serving.

BLACK-AND-WHITE COOKIES
MAKES ABOUT ABOUT 2 DOZEN

These generously iced, cakelike cookies are as cherished
by New Yorkers as bagels and cream cheese.

5	cups cake flour
1	tsp. baking powder
½	tsp. kosher salt
1¾	cups sugar
16	tbsp. unsalted butter, softened
4	eggs
1	cup milk
1	tsp. vanilla extract
1	1-lb. box confectioners' sugar, sifted
3	oz. unsweetened chocolate, finely chopped

1 Heat oven to 375°. In a large bowl, whisk together flour, baking powder, and salt; set aside. In another bowl, combine sugar and butter, and beat with an electric mixer on medium-high speed until pale and fluffy, about 3 minutes. Add eggs one at a time, beating after each addition, and beat until smooth. Add milk, vanilla, and the reserved flour mixture; beat on low speed until just combined.

2 Use an ice cream scoop or a ¼-cup measuring cup to divide the dough into roughly 24 portions. Transfer dough portions to parchment paper–lined baking sheets, spacing the portions 2" apart. Bake until cookies are set and lightly browned at the edges, about 15 minutes. Let cool completely.

3 Meanwhile, make the icing: Whisk together the confectioners' sugar and ⅓ cup boiling water in a medium glass bowl to make a smooth glaze (this will be the white icing). Working with one cookie at a time, hold the cookie horizontally, gently gripping it by the edges, and dip the top in the white glaze (you'll get some icing on your fingers); then return the cookie to the baking sheet to let the icing set. Meanwhile, make the black icing by adding the chocolate to the remaining white glaze. Microwave the mixture for about 45 seconds; stir to combine. Dip each white-glazed cookie vertically halfway into the chocolate glaze and transfer to the baking sheet. Let the chocolate glaze set completely before serving.

Baking Tip *To quicken the setting of the glazes, place the cookies in the refrigerator for about 20 minutes after each coating.*

THIN AND CHEWY
CHOCOLATE CHIP COOKIES
MAKES ABOUT 5 DOZEN

This recipe calls for more sugar and less flour than your typical ones, making for a flatter cookie that's chewy around the edges when it cools—perfect for ice cream sandwiches.

2	cups flour
1	scant tbsp. kosher salt
1¼	tsp. baking soda
1½	cups packed light brown sugar
1¼	cups sugar
16	tbsp. unsalted butter, softened
2	eggs
1	tbsp. vanilla extract
12	oz. shaved bitter-sweet chocolate
8	oz. finely ground walnuts

1 Whisk flour, salt, and baking soda in a bowl; set aside. In a separate bowl, beat sugars and butter with an electric mixer on medium speed until fluffy, 1–2 minutes. Beat in eggs one at a time. Beat in vanilla. Add reserved flour mixture, chocolate, and walnuts, and mix until just combined; refrigerate for at least 1 hour.

2 Heat oven to 325°. Using a 1 tbsp. measuring spoon, portion out and roll dough into 1" balls. Transfer balls to parchment paper–lined baking sheets, spacing dough balls 3" apart. Flatten dough balls lightly with the palm of your hand. Bake until set and lightly browned at the edges, about 15 minutes.

Baking Tip *Use the large holes of a box grater to shave the chocolate into evenly sized pieces.*

GERMAN SPICE COOKIES

(Pfeffernüsse)

MAKES 3 DOZEN

These fragrant cookies, a favorite in Germany around Christmastime,
provide a delightful rush of warm spices and holiday cheer.

½   cup honey

⅓   cup unsulfured molasses

2   tbsp. unsalted butter

2   eggs

2   cups whole wheat flour

⅓   cup almonds, finely ground

¾   tsp. ground cinnamon

¾   tsp. ground black pepper

¾   tsp. ground cloves

¾   tsp. ground cardamom

½   cup candied lemon peel, finely chopped

½   tsp. baking powder

1   cup confectioners' sugar, sifted

2   tbsp. light rum

1 Combine honey, molasses, and butter in a small pot and cook over medium-low heat, stirring constantly, until hot, 2–3 minutes. Remove from heat and let cool. Add eggs, and whisk to combine. Put flour, almonds, cinnamon, pepper, cloves, cardamom, baking powder, and half the candied lemon peel into a large bowl, and stir to combine. Add the honey mixture, and beat with a wooden spoon until well combined, to form a dough. Cover surface of dough with plastic wrap and refrigerate for 4 hours or overnight.

2 Heat oven to 350°. Form the dough into 1" balls (the dough will be very sticky). Transfer the dough balls to two parchment paper–lined baking sheets, spacing the balls 1" apart. Bake until slightly cracked on top and just firm to the touch, about 15 minutes. Transfer cookies to a wire rack and let cool slightly.

3 Meanwhile, whisk together the confectioners' sugar, rum, and 5 tsp. hot water to make a smooth glaze. Dip the tops of each cookie in the glaze, and then return them to the wire rack. While the glaze on the cookies is still moist, garnish each top with pieces of the remaining lemon peel. Set cookies aside to let cool completely.

GINGERBREAD COOKIES

MAKES ABOUT 4 DOZEN

These tasty Swedish-style Christmas cookies can be served plain or decorated with icing. This recipe comes from the famous Vete-Katten bakery in Stockholm.

3¾ cups flour

3 tsp. ground cloves

3½ tsp. ground cinnamon

2½ tsp. ground ginger

1¼ tsp. baking soda

11 tbsp. unsalted butter, softened

1 cup packed dark brown sugar

½ cup golden syrup or dark corn syrup

½ cup heavy cream

2 cups confectioners' sugar, sifted

1 tsp. fresh lemon juice

1 egg white, lightly beaten

1 In a large bowl, whisk together flour, cloves, cinnamon, ginger, and baking soda; set aside. In another large bowl, beat together butter, brown sugar, and golden syrup using a handheld mixer on medium speed until the mixture is pale and fluffy, 1–2 minutes. Add reserved flour mixture and heavy cream in 3 alternating batches, beating between each addition, and beginning and ending with the spice mixture, until the dough just comes together. Transfer dough to a work surface, divide in half, and shape each half into a flat disk. Wrap each disk in plastic wrap; refrigerate for 1 hour.

2 Heat oven to 350°. Unwrap 1 disk of dough and transfer to a floured work surface. Roll dough to a ⅛" thickness. Using cookie cutters of your choice, cut out cookies and transfer them to parchment paper–lined baking sheets, spacing the cookies 2" apart. Reroll scraps and repeat. Refrigerate the uncooked cookies for at least 20 minutes. Bake cookies, 1 sheet at a time, until browned and set, about 12 minutes. Transfer cookies to a wire rack and let cool.

3 To make the icing, whisk confectioners' sugar, lemon juice, and egg white in a medium bowl until smooth. Transfer icing to a pastry bag (or a plastic bag with its bottom corner snipped off). Pipe icing onto cookies in decorative patterns.

GINGERSNAPS
MAKES 6 DOZEN

These crunchy, wafer-thin cookies, bright with fresh ginger, really live up to their name. Eat them on their own, or crumble them on top of baked apples or pears.

1¾   cups firmly packed dark brown sugar

1½   cups (3 sticks) unsalted butter, softened

1   large egg

1   tbsp. peeled and grated fresh ginger

1½   tsp. grated lemon zest

3¾   cups all-purpose flour

2   tbsp. ground ginger

3   tsp. ground cinnamon

1¼   tsp. baking powder

½   tsp. ground white pepper

¼   tsp. ground cloves

2   tbsp. turbinado (raw) sugar

1 Using an electric mixer on medium speed, beat sugar and butter until smooth. Add egg, fresh ginger, and lemon zest, and beat well. In a bowl, whisk together flour, ground ginger, cinnamon, baking powder, white pepper, and ground cloves. Gradually add flour mixture to butter mixture, beating until well combined. Form the dough into a large disk, wrap in plastic, and refrigerate for at least 4 hours or overnight.

2 Heat the oven to 350°. Scoop out 1 tsp. of dough at a time and roll each portion into a ball. Transfer the balls to a parchment paper–lined baking sheet and flatten them into very thin rounds with the base of a flat-bottomed glass or mug that has been dipped in flour. Sprinkle the tops of the cookies with turbinado sugar and bake until crisp and browned, 8–10 minutes.

MADELEINES

MAKES ABOUT 2 DOZEN

These pretty lemon-infused sponge-cake cookies, with their distinctive scalloped pattern, are an iconic French pastry.

6	tbsp. unsalted butter, plus more for pans
1¾	cups cake flour
1	cup sugar
½	tsp. baking soda
¼	tsp. kosher salt
	Zest of 2 lemons
4	eggs, beaten

1 Heat oven to 375°. Grease two 12-mold madeleine pans. Melt butter in a pot over medium-low heat; let cool for 10 minutes. Whisk together flour, sugar, baking soda, salt, and lemon zest in a bowl; fold in eggs until the batter is smooth. Fold in the melted butter until just incorporated.

2 Divide batter between prepared pans, filling each mold about three-fourths of the way to the rim. Bake, rotating once, until madeleines are golden brown, 15–20 minutes.

Baking Tip *This recipe calls for madeleine pans with 3"-long molds. They are available at Amazon.com and many kitchenware stores.*

MAPLE WALNUT SQUARES

MAKES 9 BARS

Bakers in Quebec, Canada, make all sorts of treats using maple syrup,
the province's most famous product—among them are these chewy dessert bars,
which taste best when they're served warm from the oven and are still gooey.

8	tbsp. unsalted butter, cubed and chilled, plus more for pan
1	cup plus 2 tbsp. flour, plus more for pan
¼	cup, plus ⅔ cup maple sugar
1	cup maple syrup
1	cup chopped walnuts
¼	tsp. kosher salt
2	eggs, lightly beaten

1 Heat oven to 350°. Grease an 8" square baking pan and dust with flour; set aside. In a food processor, process butter, 1 cup of flour, and ¼ cup of maple sugar until combined; transfer to the prepared pan and press the crust evenly into the bottom of the pan. Bake until lightly browned, about 15 minutes.

2 Whisk remaining flour and maple sugar with the maple syrup, walnuts, salt, and eggs; pour the filling over the baked crust. Bake until filling is golden brown on top and set, 30–35 minutes. Let cool, and cut into squares.

MEXICAN BUTTER COOKIES

(Galletas con Chochitos)

MAKES ABOUT 3 DOZEN

Tiny ring-shaped butter cookies like these are a popular holiday treat
in Mexico, where they're typically decorated with chocolate sprinkles.

1½   cups flour

½   tsp. baking powder

¼   tsp. kosher salt

¾   cup sugar

8   tbsp. unsalted butter,
       softened

1   tsp. vanilla extract,
       preferably Mexican

3   egg yolks

1   egg white, lightly beaten

       Chocolate sprinkles,
       for decorating

1 Whisk together flour, baking powder, and salt in a bowl;
set aside. Beat together sugar, butter, and vanilla with an
electric mixer on medium speed until fluffy. Add egg yolks
one at a time, beating after each addition. Add the reserved
flour mixture, and beat until smooth.

2 Roll the dough into a 12"-long cylinder. Cut cylinder into
3 pieces; roll each piece into a thinner 12"-long cylinder.
Cut each cylinder into twelve 1"-long pieces. Roll each piece
into a ball; transfer balls to a parchment paper–lined baking
sheet. Use a flat-bottomed mug or drinking glass (dipped
in flour, if necessary) to flatten each ball into a small disk;
using your finger, poke a hole in the center of each disk.
Refrigerate dough rings for 1 hour.

3 Heat oven to 300°. Brush each ring with egg white; dip into
sprinkles to coat. Return rings to the lined baking sheets;
bake for 15 minutes.

MEXICAN CHOCOLATE
ICEBOX COOKIES

MAKES ABOUT 4 DOZEN

Perfumed with cinnamon, cayenne, and black pepper, these cookies are a
Tex-Mex specialty. Try serving them with a cup of steaming hot chocolate.

½	cup flour
¾	cup Dutch-process cocoa powder
¾	tsp. ground cinnamon
½	tsp. cayenne
¼	tsp. kosher salt
¼	tsp. freshly ground black pepper
12	tbsp. unsalted butter, softened
1	cup sugar
1½	tsp. vanilla extract
1	egg
4	oz. white chocolate

1 Whisk flour, cocoa, cinnamon, cayenne, salt, and pepper together in a medium bowl; set aside. Combine butter, sugar, and vanilla in a large bowl and beat with an electric mixer on medium-high speed until pale and fluffy, about 3 minutes. Add egg and beat until smooth. Add the reserved flour mixture and beat on low speed until just combined.

2 Heat oven to 375°. Form dough into tablespoon-size balls; place balls 2" apart on parchment paper–lined baking sheets. Bake until slightly underdone in the middle but set at the edges, about 8 minutes. Let cool completely.

3 Meanwhile, place white chocolate in a small metal bowl set over a small saucepan of simmering water over medium heat, and stir until melted and smooth. Using a fork, drizzle chocolate over each cookie to create stripes; let chocolate set before serving.

NEIMAN MARCUS COOKIES

MAKES ABOUT 4½ DOZEN

This beloved recipe didn't originate at the namesake department store,
but rather in the kitchen of an unknown cook, probably in the 1940s,
when the now-famous legend of a $250 Neiman Marcus chocolate chip
cookie recipe first began to circulate.

16	tbsp. unsalted butter
1	cup sugar
1	cup packed light brown sugar
1	tsp. vanilla extract
2	eggs
2½	cups rolled oats, finely ground in a food processor
2	cups flour
1	tsp. baking powder
1	tsp. baking soda
½	tsp. kosher salt
2	cups semisweet chocolate chips
4	oz. milk chocolate, finely chopped
1½	cups walnuts, roughly chopped

1 Heat oven to 375°. Using a hand mixer, beat butter and sugars together in a large bowl until fluffy, about 3 minutes. Add vanilla and eggs, and beat until combined, about 30 seconds. Add oats, flour, baking powder, baking soda, and salt, and beat until combined, about 30 seconds. Stir in both chocolates and walnuts.

2 Roll dough into 1½" balls and place them 2" apart on parchment paper–lined baking sheets. Bake until light golden brown but still soft in the middle, 10–12 minutes.

NORWEGIAN WAFER COOKIES

(Krumkakes)

MAKES ABOUT 2 DOZEN

These whipped-cream-filled wafer cookies, a Christmastime treat in Norway, are made on a special griddle that imprints an intricate design.

1	cup sugar
4	eggs
9	tbsp. unsalted butter, melted and cooled
1	tsp. ground cardamom
½	tsp. vanilla extract
1½	cups flour
2	tbsp. baking powder
	Sweetened whipped cream, to fill cookies
	Confectioners' sugar, to garnish

1 In a bowl, whisk together sugar and eggs. Whisk in 8 tbsp. of the butter, the cardamom, and the vanilla. Sift flour and baking powder into batter; whisk batter until smooth.

2 Heat a krumkake maker (see below), and brush the surface of the molds with remaining butter. Add 1 heaping tbsp. batter to each mold. Close cover, and cook until wafers are golden, 45–50 seconds. Remove wafers from molds and, working quickly so that the wafers don't become brittle, wrap them around a cone-shaped roller (see below); let harden. Remove from roller. Repeat with remaining batter, and let cones cool.

3 Right before serving, pipe the whipped cream into the rolled wafer cookies, and dust with confectioners' sugar.

Baking Tip *To make these cookies, you'll need a krumkake griddle and a cone-shaped mold or roller. We suggest the CucinaPro 220-02 Krumkake Baker and a wooden krumkake or ice cream cone mold, both available at Amazon.com.*

NICK'S SUPERNATURAL BROWNIES

MAKES ABOUT 2 DOZEN

This recipe for incredibly moist and fudgy brownies comes from
the acclaimed baker and cookbook author Nick Malgieri.

16 tbsp. unsalted butter,
plus more for greasing

8 oz. bittersweet chocolate,
cut into ¼" pieces

4 eggs

1 cup sugar

1 cup packed dark
brown sugar

2 tsp. vanilla extract

½ tsp. kosher salt

1 cup flour

1 Heat oven to 350°. Grease a 9" x 13" baking pan and
line with parchment paper; grease the parchment paper
too. Set pan aside.

2 Pour enough water into a 4-quart saucepan that it
reaches a depth of 1". Bring to a boil; reduce heat to low.
Combine butter and chocolate in a medium bowl; set bowl
over saucepan. Cook, stirring, until melted and smooth,
about 5 minutes. Remove from heat; set aside.

3 Whisk eggs in a large bowl. Add both sugars, vanilla, and
salt; whisk thoroughly. Stir in reserved chocolate mixture;
fold in flour. Pour batter into the prepared pan, and spread
evenly. Bake until a toothpick inserted into the center comes
out clean, 30–35 minutes. Let cool completely before cutting
into squares.

Baking Tip *To achieve a shiny, crackly-crisp crust on top,
whisk the eggs and sugars together for at least 3 minutes.*

ORANGE MERINGUE KISSES

MAKES ABOUT 2 DOZEN

As delicious as they are pretty, these airy and elegant sandwich
cookies are the perfect topper to a big holiday meal.

¾   cup sugar

4   egg whites

2   tsp. orange extract

10   drops yellow food
coloring

2   drops red food coloring

6   oz. white chocolate,
melted and cooled

1 Heat oven to 200°. Whisk sugar and egg whites together
in a bowl set over a pan of simmering water; stir constantly
until mixture reaches 140° on an instant-read thermometer.
Remove bowl from pan, and, using a hand mixer, beat
on high speed until cooled, about 6 minutes. Add orange
extract and food colorings, and beat until evenly combined.
Transfer meringue mixture to a piping bag fitted with a ⅜"
star tip, and pipe 1"-wide kisses on a parchment paper–lined
baking sheet. Bake until meringues are crisp and dry to the
touch, about 2 hours. Turn oven off and let meringues cool
completely in oven.

2 Dip the bottom of a meringue kiss in the melted white
chocolate and press the bottom of a second meringue
kiss onto the first to make a sandwich. Repeat with
remaining meringues and white chocolate. Let chocolate
set before serving.

Baking Tip *Substitute other fruit extracts and colorings
to produce a variety of different meringues: mint with green
coloring, for example, or cinnamon with red coloring.*

PEANUT BUTTER COOKIES

MAKES ABOUT 2½ DOZEN

These old-school cookies deliver pure pleasure and comfort. Use a creamy supermarket-brand peanut butter like original Jif or Skippy, since most peanut butters labeled "natural" don't take well to baking.

3	cups flour
2½	tsp. baking powder
1	cup sugar
1	cup packed dark brown sugar
12	tbsp. unsalted butter, softened
2	eggs
1	cup peanut butter
2	tsp. vanilla extract

1 Heat oven to 350°. Whisk together flour and baking powder; set aside. In a large bowl, beat sugars and butter together with a hand mixer until pale and fluffy, about 3 minutes. Add eggs one at a time, beating well after each addition, until smooth. Add peanut butter and vanilla, and beat until smooth. Add reserved flour mixture, and beat until just combined.

2 Using a tablespoon, portion out dough and roll into 1" balls; place balls 2" apart on a parchment paper–lined baking sheet. Gently press the tines of a fork into the surface of the dough balls to flatten them slightly and create a crosshatch pattern. Bake, rotating baking sheet front to back halfway through cooking, until cookies are golden brown and barely set, about 14 minutes. Let cool before serving.

Baking Tip *If your fork begins sticking to the cookie balls when you're making the crosshatch pattern, just dip it in flour.*

PECAN SHORTBREADS

(Polvorones)

MAKES ABOUT 4 DOZEN

Finely ground pecans and *canela*—a close cousin of cinnamon—flavor these delicate, crumbly cookies, a popular sweet all over Mexico.

¾	cup pecans
¾	cup sugar
1½	cups flour
1	tsp. Mexican *canela* or ground cinnamon
½	tsp. kosher salt
6	tbsp. unsalted butter, softened
1½	tsp. vanilla extract, preferably Mexican
1	cup confectioners' sugar

1 Combine pecans and ¼ cup of the sugar in a food processor, and process until pecans are very finely ground, about 30 seconds. Add remaining sugar along with flour, cinnamon, and salt, and pulse until evenly incorporated. Add butter and vanilla, and process until dough just comes together and forms a ball. Transfer dough ball to a lightly floured work surface, and form into a disk; wrap in plastic wrap, and refrigerate for 1 hour. Meanwhile, place confectioners' sugar in a large bowl; set aside.

2 Heat oven to 350°. Transfer dough disk to a work surface, and, using a rolling pin, roll dough to a ½" thickness. Using a 1¼" round cookie cutter, cut out dough rounds and transfer them to parchment paper–lined baking sheets, spacing the dough rounds 2" apart. Reroll dough scraps and cut out more dough rounds; transfer them to the baking sheet. Chill dough rounds for 30 minutes.

3 Bake, rotating baking sheets front to back and top to bottom halfway through baking, until cookies are lightly browned and set, about 14 minutes. Let cool for 10 minutes, and then transfer cookies to a bowl of confectioners' sugar; toss gently to coat the cookies evenly in sugar.

Baking Tip *If you can't find Mexican canela and Mexican vanilla extract, regular supermarket cinnamon and vanilla will work just fine.*

PECAN SQUARES

MAKES ABOUT 5 DOZEN

These soft, rich, and chewy cookies, a take on pecan pie, make a great
substitute for that dessert after a big holiday meal.

FOR THE CRUST:

3	cups flour
1	tsp. baking powder
½	tsp. kosher salt
10	tbsp. unsalted butter, softened
6	tbsp. vegetable shortening
¾	cup sugar
2	eggs
½	tsp. vanilla extract

FOR THE TOPPING:

16	tbsp. unsalted butter
½	cup honey
¼	cup sugar
1¼	cups light brown sugar
¼	cup heavy cream
4	cups chopped pecans

1 Make the crust: Combine flour, baking powder, and salt
in a medium bowl and mix well; set aside. Beat butter and
shortening with a hand mixer on medium speed until
smooth. Gradually add sugar, and beat until mixture is light
and fluffy. Beat in eggs and vanilla, then reduce speed and
add the reserved flour mixture, mixing until just combined.

2 Gather dough into a ball, flatten slightly, and then, using
your fingers, press dough into a parchment paper–lined
10" x 15" jelly roll pan. Refrigerate uncooked crust until firm,
about 30 minutes.

3 Heat oven to 375°. Prick crust all over with a fork, then bake
until golden brown, about 15 minutes. Set aside to let cool.

4 Make the topping: Combine butter, honey, and sugars in
a 2-qt. saucepan. Simmer, stirring constantly, over medium
heat until sugars dissolve and mixture darkens and foams,
5 minutes. Remove from heat, whisk in the cream, and stir
in the pecans.

5 Spread the topping evenly over the crust and bake until
topping is bubbly, about 15 minutes. Remove pan from
oven and let cool completely on a wire rack before cutting
into squares.

PINE NUT COOKIES

(Pignoli)

MAKES ABOUT 3 DOZEN

A sprinkling of pine nuts gives these classic Italian almond-meringue cookies an extra layer of nutty flavor.

2 cups whole blanched almonds

½ cup sugar

1 cup confectioners' sugar

3 egg whites, lightly beaten

½ cup pine nuts

1 Heat oven to 300°. Combine almonds and granulated sugar in a food processor, and process until almonds are very finely ground, about 4 minutes. Add confectioners' sugar and egg whites, and process until a smooth dough forms.

2 Transfer dough to a piping bag fitted with a ½" round tip, and pipe 1½" circles onto parchment paper–lined baking sheets, spacing the circles 2" apart. Gently press 10–12 pine nuts into the top of each mound.

3 Bake, rotating baking sheets top to bottom and front to back halfway through cooking, until cookies are golden brown, about 25 minutes. Let cool completely before serving.

SNICKERDOODLES

MAKES ABOUT 4 DOZEN

These soft, chewy cookies, rich with butter and rolled in
cinnamon sugar, deliver pure pleasure and comfort.

3	cups flour
2	tsp. cream of tartar
1	tsp. baking soda
¼	tsp. kosher salt
1¾	cups sugar
16	tbsp. unsalted butter, softened
1½	tsp. vanilla extract
5	tsp. ground cinnamon
2	eggs

1 In a medium bowl, whisk together flour, cream of tartar, baking soda, and salt; set aside. Using a handheld mixer on medium speed, beat 1½ cups of sugar and butter together in a medium bowl until pale and fluffy, 2 minutes. Add vanilla and 2 tsp. of cinnamon; beat for 1 minute more. Add eggs one at a time, beating well after each addition. Add reserved flour mixture; mix on low speed until just combined. Refrigerate dough for 30 minutes.

2 Heat oven to 375°. Combine remaining sugar and cinnamon in a small bowl. Remove dough from refrigerator and, using a 1-tbsp. measuring spoon, portion the dough and roll into 1" balls. Roll each ball in the cinnamon-sugar mixture to coat. Arrange dough balls 2" apart on parchment paper–lined baking sheets. Bake until golden brown, about 10 minutes.

POPPY SEED HONEY COOKIES

(Pirishkes)

MAKES ABOUT 5½ DOZEN

Though less widely known than rugelach and hamantaschen, these scrumptious honey-coated cookies deserve a high place in the pantheon of Jewish desserts.

3   cups flour

¼   cup poppy seeds

2   tsp. baking powder

1   tsp. kosher salt

¾   cup sugar

8   tbsp. unsalted butter, softened

1   tsp. vanilla extract

2   eggs

1   cup honey

1 Heat oven to 350°. Whisk flour, poppy seeds, baking powder, and salt in a bowl; set aside. Beat sugar, butter, and vanilla in a bowl with a hand mixer until pale and fluffy. Add eggs one at a time, beating after each addition; add the reserved flour mixture and mix until a dough forms. Shape the dough into a disk, and cut it in half. Using a rolling pin, roll each dough portion between sheets of parchment paper until ¼" thick; slide the rolled dough pieces, keeping them between the sheets of parchment paper, onto a baking sheet, and refrigerate until firm, about 30 minutes. Remove the parchment paper, and, using a pizza cutter or pastry wheel, cut out 1½"-wide diamonds from the dough; transfer them to parchment paper–lined baking sheets. Bake until light golden brown, 12–15 minutes.

2 Meanwhile, bring the honey and ⅓ cup water to a boil in a small saucepan; continue cooking until honey has thinned, about 2 minutes. Arrange the cookies in a single layer on a rimmed baking sheet, and pour honey over them until they're evenly coated. Let sit for 10 minutes before serving.

Baking Tip *You'll get more uniform-looking cookies if you use a ruler as your guide when you're cutting the diamond shapes from the dough.*

PLUM STRUDEL BARS

MAKES 1 DOZEN

Nuts and fruit preserves are key ingredients in many Jewish desserts,
including these delectable walnut-and-plum cookies.

2	cups flour
½	cup sugar
4	tbsp. unsalted butter, cut into ½" cubes and chilled
1½	tsp. baking powder
½	tsp. kosher salt
2	lightly beaten eggs, plus 1 more for brushing
1	cup walnuts
1	12-oz. jar plum preserves

1 Combine flour, ¼ cup of sugar, butter, baking powder, and salt in the bowl of a food processor, and process until pea-size crumbs form. Add 2 eggs and ¼ cup ice-cold water; pulse until a dough forms. Form dough into a disk; wrap in plastic wrap and refrigerate for 1 hour. Combine the remaining sugar and the walnuts in the bowl of a food processor, and process until nuts are finely chopped; set aside.

2 Add plum preserves to the bowl of the food processor, and puree until smooth; set aside.

3 Heat oven to 375°. Cut the dough disk into thirds; roll each portion into an 11" x 7" rectangle. Lay one of the dough rectangles into the bottom of an 11" x 7" baking dish. Spread half the preserves over the top of the dough, and then sprinkle with ⅓ of the walnuts. Lay a second dough rectangle over the first and top it with the remaining preserves and half of the remaining walnuts. Finally, lay the third dough rectangle over the second, and prick with tines of a fork.

4 Brush top of dough with remaining egg; sprinkle with remaining walnuts. Bake until golden brown, 25–30 minutes. Let cool completely before cutting into squares or bars.

RAINBOW COOKIES

MAKES ABOUT 10 DOZEN

These moist, cakelike layered treats make a colorful
addition to a holiday cookie tray.

1½ cups unsalted butter,
softened, plus more
for pans

2 cups flour, plus more
for pans

1 cup sugar

1 12.5-oz. can almond
pastry filling, such
as Solo brand

4 eggs

12 drops green food coloring

12 drops red food coloring

12 drops yellow food
coloring

1 12-oz. jar seedless
raspberry jam

12 oz. semisweet chocolate,
melted

1 Heat oven to 350°. Grease three 9" x 13" baking pans, dust
them with flour, and line them with parchment paper; set
aside. Using a hand mixer on high speed, beat butter and
sugar in a bowl until pale and fluffy, about 2 minutes. Add
pastry filling; beat until smooth. Add eggs one at a time,
beating well after each addition. Add flour; beat until just
combined. Evenly divide batter into 3 bowls. Add green food
coloring to one bowl, red food coloring to the second bowl,
and yellow food coloring to the third bowl; stir colorings
into batters. Using an offset spatula, spread each batter as
smoothly and evenly as possible into a prepared baking pan.
Bake the cakes until just beginning to brown on top, about
10 minutes. Let cool, and then invert cakes onto wire racks.

2 Heat jam in a 1-qt. saucepan over medium heat, stirring,
until smooth; let cool slightly. Place green cake on a cutting
board or foil-lined baking sheet. Using an offset spatula,
spread half the jam over the green cake; top with the yellow
cake. Spread the remaining jam over the yellow cake; top
with the red cake. Refrigerate for at least 1 hour.

3 Trim cake edges to form an even-sided block. Slice the
block crosswise into 1½"-wide segments; transfer the segments
to a cutting board. Using an offset spatula, spread chocolate
over top, sides, and ends of each segment until completely
covered; refrigerate until chocolate is set. Slice each segment
crosswise into squares and serve.

Baking Tip *Because these cakes are so thin, use an offset
spatula to help you spread the batter into the pans evenly,
as it will not even out while it bakes.*

SAFFRON BISCOTTI

MAKES ABOUT 3½ DOZEN

Saffron, with its warm and earthy flavors, is a prized ingredient in many Swedish baked treats, including these dainty biscotti, which are shorter and fatter than their typical Italian counterparts.

3	cups flour
2	tsp. baking powder
½	tsp. kosher salt
1	cup sugar
4	tbsp. unsalted butter, softened
1	tbsp. orange zest
1	tsp. saffron, lightly crushed
2	eggs
¼	cup milk
4	oz. dark chocolate, chopped
4	tbsp. pearl sugar, to garnish

1 Heat oven to 325°. Whisk together flour, baking powder, and salt in a medium bowl; set aside. In a large bowl, using a handheld mixer on medium speed, beat together sugar, butter, orange zest, and saffron until mixture is pale and fluffy, 1–2 minutes. Add the eggs one at a time, beating well after each addition; add milk, and mix until combined. Reduce mixer speed to low, and add the reserved flour mixture in 3 parts, mixing briefly after each addition. Continue mixing until just combined. Mix in chocolate, then transfer dough to a work surface.

2 Divide dough into four equal portions, and transfer each portion to its own parchment paper–lined baking sheet. Form each portion into a 12" x 1" flattened log; sprinkle each log with 1 tbsp. pearl sugar and refrigerate for 20 minutes. Bake, 1 sheet at a time, until biscotti segments are lightly browned around edges, 30–35 minutes. Transfer baking sheet to a wire rack and let cool for 15 minutes.

3 Reduce oven temperature to 300°. Transfer each 12" biscotti segment to a cutting board and, using a serrated knife, slice the segments into 1"-wide pieces to make tiny individual biscotti. Return sliced biscotti to the baking sheet, cut sides up and spaced evenly apart. Bake, 1 sheet at a time, until light brown and dry to the touch, 15–20 minutes. Transfer to a wire rack to let cool completely before serving.

SPRINKLE COOKIES

MAKES ABOUT 3 DOZEN

Around the holidays, Italian bakeries stock their shelves
with dozens of festive, colorful cookies like these.

1½	cups flour, plus more as needed
1½	tsp. baking powder
½	tsp. kosher salt
12	tbsp. unsalted butter, softened
¾	cup sugar
1	egg
2	tsp. vanilla extract
	Zest of ½ lemon
1	egg white, lightly beaten
½	cup multicolored sprinkles

1 Whisk together flour, baking powder, and salt in a bowl; set aside. Beat butter and sugar with an electric mixer on medium-high speed until pale and fluffy, about 2 minutes. Add egg, vanilla, and lemon zest, and beat until smooth; add the reserved flour mixture, and beat until just combined. Using a 1-oz. ice cream scoop or 2 tablespoons, portion and shape dough into 1" balls; place balls 2" apart on a parchment paper–lined baking sheet. Lightly flour the bottom of a ¼-cup measuring cup, and press each ball into a flat disk; refrigerate disks for 30 minutes.

2 Heat oven to 375°. Place sprinkles in a bowl; set aside. Using a pastry brush, lightly brush tops of disks with egg white and then press the top of each disk into the sprinkles. Return disks to baking sheets, and bake, rotating baking sheets top to bottom and front to back halfway through cooking, until cookies are set and lightly browned on the bottom, about 10 minutes. Let cool before serving.

DUTCH GINGER COOKIES

(Speculaas)

MAKES ABOUT 2 DOZEN

Ginger cookies baked in intricate molds are a cherished Christmas tradition in the Netherlands and Flemish-speaking Belgium.

3 cups flour, plus more for molds

2 tsp. ground cinnamon

1½ tsp. freshly grated nutmeg

1 tsp. ground coriander

1 tsp. ground ginger

½ tsp. ground cloves

½ tsp. baking soda

½ tsp. kosher salt

¼ tsp. freshly ground white pepper

12 tbsp. unsalted butter, softened

1 cup packed light brown sugar

⅓ cup milk

1 In a bowl, whisk together flour, cinnamon, nutmeg, coriander, ginger, cloves, baking soda, salt, and white pepper; set aside. In an electric mixer, beat together butter and sugar. Add half the flour mixture, and mix until smooth. Add milk and remaining flour mixture, and mix until smooth. Form the dough into 2 disks, and wrap each in plastic wrap. Refrigerate for 2 hours.

2 Heat oven to 350°. Working with 1 disk at a time, pull off a small handful of dough and press it into a floured speculaas mold (see below); scrape away excess dough and invert the mold to free the molded cookie. Brush away flour from molded cookie. Repeat with remaining dough. (If you don't have a speculaas mold, you can simply roll the dough disks to a ¼" thickness and then cut them into 2" x 3" rectangles.) Transfer the molded cookies to parchment paper–lined baking sheets, spacing cookies 2" apart. Bake until golden brown, 16–18 minutes.

Baking Tip *Speculaas molds can be purchased at eBay.com, Etsy.com, HollandsBest.com, or other specialty online retailers. Be sure to dust the molds generously with flour before each use to keep the cookies from sticking.*

DREAM COOKIES

(Drömkakor)

MAKES ABOUT 4 DOZEN

These airy, melt-in-your-mouth butter cookies are
a holiday tradition in many Swedish homes.

1⅔   cups flour

1   tsp. baking soda

8   tbsp. unsalted butter,
    softened

1¼   cups sugar

1   tbsp. vanilla sugar (or
    1½ tsp. vanilla extract)

⅓   cup canola oil

1 Heat oven to 300°. In a small bowl, whisk together
flour and baking soda; set aside. In a large bowl, beat butter
and sugars with a hand mixer on medium speed until pale
and fluffy, about 1–2 minutes. Add oil, and mix until smooth.
Add reserved flour mixture, and stir until just combined.

2 Using a tablespoon-size measuring spoon, portion and
shape the dough into 1" balls. Place the dough balls 2" apart
on baking sheets lined with parchment paper. Bake the
cookies, putting just one sheet in the oven at a time, until
they start to crack on top and are very lightly browned,
about 25 minutes. Transfer cookies to a wire rack and let
cool before serving. Repeat with remaining sheets.

ALMOND-CREAM TARTLETS

MAKES 32 TARTLETS

For these sophisticated yet simple desserts, whipped cream and
a colorful berry sauce fill a rich almond pastry crust.

½ cup whole blanched
    almonds

1¾ cups sugar

2⅓ cups flour

15 tbsp. unsalted butter,
    softened, plus more
    for pan

1   cup fresh or frozen
    lingonberries or
    cranberries

1   tbsp. fresh orange juice

1½ cups heavy cream

2   tsp. vanilla extract

1 Make the pastry dough: Add almonds to the bowl of a food
processor and process until finely chopped. Add ¾ cup of the
sugar, and process until very finely ground. Add the flour,
and pulse until combined. Add the butter, and pulse until
the dough begins to come together. Transfer dough to a work
surface and knead briefly until smooth.

2 Heat oven to 400°. Divide dough into 32 equal pieces,
about 1 oz. each. Press each dough piece into a 2-oz.,
1⅞" x 1⅜" clamshell-shaped baking tin (see below). Trim
away any loose edges and transfer molded pastry crust to
a rimmed baking sheet lined with parchment paper. Repeat
with remaining dough pieces. Refrigerate the uncooked
crusts for 30 minutes. Prick the bottom of each pastry crust
with a fork, and bake until golden and set, 12–14 minutes.
Transfer to a wire rack and let cool completely.

3 Heat ¼ cup of the sugar, the lingonberries, and the orange
juice in a 1-qt. saucepan over medium heat. Cook, stirring
frequently, until berries break down and sugar dissolves,
about 10 minutes. Set aside to let cool completely. In a large
bowl, whisk the heavy cream and vanilla until soft peaks
form; slowly add remaining sugar to cream and beat until stiff
peaks form. Refrigerate whipped cream until ready to use.

4 To serve, fill each cooled pastry crust with a heaping
tablespoon of the whipped cream, and top with a teaspoon
of the berry sauce.

Baking Tip *If you don't own clamshell-shaped pastry tins,
you can use almost any two-ounce baking mold to shape the
pastry crusts.*

SWISS RASPBERRY SANDWICH COOKIES

(Spitzbuebe)

MAKES ABOUT 3 DOZEN

The very picture of old-world elegance, these delicate, buttery cookies
are filled with a thin layer of raspberry preserves.

1½ cups (3 sticks) unsalted butter, softened

2 cups confectioners' sugar

3 egg yolks

3½ cups flour

1 cup seedless raspberry preserves

1 Beat butter and 1½ cups of the sugar in a large bowl with an electric mixer on medium speed until light and fluffy. Add the egg yolks, and beat until smooth. Add the flour, and beat until just combined. Form the dough into a 9" x 11" rectangle and wrap tightly with plastic wrap. Refrigerate for 1 hour.

2 Heat oven to 325°. Divide chilled dough into 6 equal portions. Rewrap 5 of the portions individually in plastic wrap and refrigerate. (This will ensure the dough is cold when you're working with it.) On a lightly floured surface, roll the remaining dough piece into a 9" square. Using a 3" round cookie cutter, cut out 9 rounds of dough and transfer them to a parchment paper–lined baking sheet, spacing rounds about 1" apart; reserve scraps. Repeat the process with the remaining chilled dough pieces and additional baking sheets. Combine all the leftover scraps into a ball, roll dough ball flat, and cut more circles; transfer to lined baking sheet. Using a 1¼" round cookie cutter, cut a hole in the center of half of the circles (these will become the tops of the cookies). Bake all the dough circles in batches, rotating pans halfway through, until pale golden brown, about 15 minutes per batch. Let cookies cool completely.

3 Heat preserves in a 2-qt. saucepan over medium heat, and simmer, stirring, until thickened and reduced by about one-quarter, about 5 minutes. Transfer preserves to a bowl; let cool. Place remaining ½ cup sugar into a fine strainer; dust cookie tops. Flip the rounds without holes upside down, and spoon about ½ tsp. of the preserves onto each. Using a small spatula, spread preserves to within ⅛" of the edges. Cover each with a cookie top. Transfer remaining preserves to a plastic bag; snip a corner. Pipe a small amount of preserves into each hole.

VANILLA CRESCENTS

(Vanillekipferl)

MAKES ABOUT 4 DOZEN

Akin to Mexican wedding cookies and Greek *kourabiedes*, these sugar-dusted Austrian treats are typically served during the weeks leading up to Christmas.

1 cup confectioners' sugar, plus more for dusting

16 tbsp. unsalted butter, softened

2 tsp. vanilla extract

5 oz. walnuts, finely ground in a food processor

2½ cups flour, plus more for rolling

1 Beat together sugar, butter, and vanilla on medium speed of a hand mixer in a bowl; add nuts and flour, and mix until smooth. Transfer dough to a lightly floured work surface and divide into quarters. Roll each quarter into a cylinder; divide each cylinder into 12 pieces.

2 Roll each piece into a sausage shape. Taper the ends, and bend piece into a crescent. Transfer crescents to parchment paper–lined baking sheets, spacing the crescents 1" apart. Refrigerate for 30 minutes.

3 Heat oven to 325°. Bake crescents, one baking sheet at a time, until golden brown, 12–15 minutes. Let the cookies cool completely, and, using a sifter or fine strainer, dust them with confectioners' sugar.

TABLE OF EQUIVALENTS

The exact equivalents in the following tables have been rounded for convenience.

Liquid and Dry Measurements

U.S.	METRIC
¼ teaspoon	1.25 milliliters
½ teaspoon	2.5 milliliters
1 teaspoon	5 milliliters
1 tablespoon (3 teaspoons)	15 milliliters
1 fluid ounce	30 milliliters
¼ cup	65 milliliters
⅓ cup	80 milliliters
1 cup	235 milliliters
1 pint (2 cups)	480 milliliters
1 quart (4 cups, 32 fluid ounces)	950 milliliters
1 gallon (4 quarts)	3.8 liters
1 ounce (by weight)	28 grams
1 pound	454 grams
2.2 pounds	1 kilogram

Length Measures

U.S.	METRIC
⅛ inch	3 millimeters
¼ inch	6 millimeters
½ inch	12 millimeters
1 inch	2.5 centimeters

Oven Temperatures

FAHRENHEIT	CELSIUS	GAS
250°	120°	½
275°	140°	1
300°	150°	2
325°	160°	3
350°	180°	4
375°	190°	5
400°	200°	6
425°	220°	7
450°	230°	8
475°	240°	9
500°	260°	10

INDEX

ACKNOWLEDGMENTS

I would like to thank all the people involved with making this book happen. David McAninch oversaw the editing of the project and kept me laughing throughout. The regular SAVEUR team—Beth Kracklauer, Betsy Andrews, Gabriella Gershenson, Karen Shimizu, Chelsea Pomales, Felicia Campbell, and Greg Ferro—also kept things lighthearted as they worked on yet another book project. Dave Weaver was once again able to weave the photographs and edit together masterfully as he created a design that is almost as fun as making cookies. And our test kitchen continues to come through in the clutch: Ben Mims and Kellie Evans took extremely complicated recipes and made them accessible to anyone who cares to try them; and Todd Coleman not only oversaw their efforts, he also shot most of the images that appear on these pages. I'd also like to thank our colleagues at Weldon Owen—Hannah Rahill, Amy Marr, Emma Boys, Lauren Charles, Rachel Lopez Metzger and Jennifer Newens—who have been such a pleasure to work with, even when we're making changes to our changes. *—James Oseland, Editor-in-Chief*

PHOTOGRAPHY CREDITS

Andre Baranowski, page 2; **Nicole Franzen,** page 95; **Maxime Iattoni,** pages 13, 17, 21, 28, 31, 35, 38, 51, 74, 78, 89, 99; **Todd Coleman,** all others.

ISBN 13: 978-1-61628-603-3
ISBN 10: 1-61628-603-2

Design by Dave Weaver

Conceived and produced with SAVEUR by Weldon Owen Inc.
415 Jackson Street, Suite 200, San Francisco, CA 94111
Telephone: 415 291 0100 Fax: 415 291 8841

SAVEUR and Weldon Owen are divisions of **BONNIER**